ISO 27001/ISO 27002

A guide to information security management systems

ISO 27001/ISO 27002

A guide to information security management systems

ALAN CALDER

IT Governance Publishing

Every possible effort has been made to ensure that the information contained in this book is accurate at the time of going to press, and the publisher and the author cannot accept responsibility for any errors or omissions, however caused. Any opinions expressed in this book are those of the author, not the publisher. Websites identified are for reference only, not endorsement, and any website visits are at the reader's own risk. No responsibility for loss or damage occasioned to any person acting, or refraining from action, as a result of the material in this publication can be accepted by the publisher or the author.

Apart from any fair dealing for the purposes of research or private study, or criticism or review, as permitted under the Copyright, Designs and Patents Act 1988, this publication may only be reproduced, stored or transmitted, in any form, or by any means, with the prior permission in writing of the publisher or, in the case of reprographic reproduction, in accordance with the terms of licences issued by the Copyright Licensing Agency. Enquiries concerning reproduction outside those terms should be sent to the publisher at the following address:

IT Governance Publishing Ltd
Unit 3, Clive Court
Bartholomew's Walk
Cambridgeshire Business Park
Ely, Cambridgeshire
CB7 4EA
United Kingdom
www.itgovernancepublishing.co.uk

First edition published in the United Kingdom in 2023 by IT Governance Publishing.

ISBN 978-1-78778-493-2

Cover image originally sourced from Shutterstock®.

ABOUT THE AUTHOR

Alan Calder is the Group CEO of GRC International Group PLC, the AIM-listed company that owns IT Governance Ltd. Alan is an acknowledged international cyber security guru, and a leading author on information security and IT governance issues. He has been involved in the development of a wide range of information security management training courses that have been accredited by International Board for IT Governance Qualifications (IBITGQ). Alan has consulted for clients across the globe and is a regular media commentator and speaker.

ACKNOWLEDGEMENTS

I would like to Stuart Griffin, Technical Writer at GRC International Group PLC, for his help developing the material in this book.

CONTENTS

INTRODUCTION

Information is the lifeblood of the modern world. It is at the heart of our personal and working lives, yet all too often control of that information is in the hands of organisations, not people. As a result, there is ever-increasing pressure on those organisations to ensure that the information they hold is adequately protected. All over the world, governments and regulatory bodies are focused on implementing laws and regulations that mandate effective information security and cyber resilience measures, with harsh penalties for those that fail to uphold their obligations.

Demonstrating that an organisation is a responsible custodian of information is not simply a matter of complying with the law – it has become a defining factor in an organisation's success or failure. The negative publicity and loss of trust associated with data breaches and cyber attacks can seriously impact customer retention and business opportunities, while an increasing number of tender opportunities are only open to those with independently certified information security measures.

With more than 70,000 certifications across the globe, ISO 27001 is one of the leading information security standards.[1] It offers an internationally recognised route for organisations of all sizes and industries to adopt and

---

[1] International Organization for Standardization (ISO), *The ISO Survey 2022*, September 2023, *https://www.iso.org/the-iso-survey.html*.

demonstrate effective, independently verified information security. An ISO 27001-compliant information security management system (ISMS) takes a whole-organisation, risk-based approach that addresses people, processes and technology – the three pillars of information security – backed up by continual improvement to ensure that security measures and risk assessments keep pace with the fast-changing cyber threat landscape.

A brief history of ISO 27001

The earliest incarnation of what would become ISO 27001 was a British standard: BS 7799. Published in 1995, it contained a code of practice for information security and a list of information security controls that organisations could use. BS 7799 was substantially revised over the next few years and in 1999, it was republished as a two-part set. The first part (BS 7799-1) contained a revised version of the original code of practice and set of controls, and the second part (BS 7799-2) defined a specification for an ISMS based on a selection of those controls supported by a management framework.

Several years later, the specification for an ISMS outlined in BS 7799-2 was formally adopted by the International Organization for Standardization (ISO) and republished in 2005 as ISO/IEC 27001:2005 *Information technology — Security techniques — Information security management systems — Requirements*. The code of practice and set of controls were published as a companion standard, ISO 27002:2005 *Information technology — Security techniques — Code of practice for information security management*.

Since then, both ISO 27001 and ISO 27002 have undergone two major revisions. New editions of each were published in 2013, and again in 2022.

The ISO 27000 family

ISO 27001 and ISO 27002 are part of a family of ISO standards that address ISMSs and their related aspects. There are more than 50 standards in the family, but organisations will use only a fraction of these when implementing their ISMS.

The core standards in the family are ISO 27000, ISO 27001 and ISO 27002. ISO 27000 provides an overview of an ISMS and how it functions, alongside definitions of key terms and explanations of some fundamental principles. ISO 27001 provides the specification for an ISMS and a list of key information security controls, and is the standard against which ISMSs are certified. ISO 27002 provides detailed guidance on the information security controls described in ISO 27001.

Organisations that implement an ISO 27001-compliant ISMS will need these three standards to do so successfully. The rest of the family provide additional guidance for specific aspects of the ISMS, or additional requirements for 'add-ons' that expand the remit of the ISMS to cover specific subject areas.

For example, ISO 27004 provides guidance on monitoring, measurement, analysis and evaluation for an ISMS, while ISO 27005 (which was also updated in 2022) provides detailed guidance on information security risk management. ISO 27033 is a series of standards that address network security, while the ISO 27034 series is dedicated to application security.

Two of the most popular 'add-on' standards are ISO 27018 and ISO 27701. ISO 27018 is a code of practice for the protection of personally identifiable information (PII) in public Cloud services, while ISO 27701 provides guidelines and requirements for privacy information (i.e. PII) management within an ISMS.

With the ever-increasing popularity of Cloud services in business and the trend towards greater and more exacting privacy legislation worldwide following the EU General Data Protection Regulation (GDPR) in 2018, more and more organisations are using ISO 27018 and ISO 27701 to help them comply with that legislation. Both the UK and EU GDPR, for example, obligate organisations to take appropriate technical and organisational measures to protect personal information. An ISO 27001-compliant ISMS supported by ISO 27701 offers an excellent way of demonstrating that.

ISO 27001:2022 and ISO 27002:2022 updates

All ISO standards are periodically reviewed and updated. This process usually takes about five years, though sometimes longer if the subject matter is complex or the pace of change in the relevant industry or associated technologies is relatively fast.

New editions of ISO 27001 and ISO 27002 were published in 2022, replacing the 2013 editions of both standards. Organisations that are already certified to ISO 27001:2013 have three years from publication to transition their ISMS to the 2022 edition. However, certification bodies will stop offering recertification to ISO 27001:2013 by 30 April 2024, so organisations with a certificate that expires after that date will be obliged to transition before the 31 October 2025 deadline.

Many of the changes in the 2022 edition of ISO 27001 are relatively minor, aligning the core text of the Standard to the latest (2021) revision of Annex SL or clarifying areas that were previously unclear.[2] There is one new, relatively broad requirement to plan changes to the ISMS (Clause 6.3), but the major changes are found in Annex A.

Annex A contains a list of core information security controls that are applicable to every organisation. These controls are explained in more detail in ISO 27002, which also provides implementation guidance and supporting information. Annex A and ISO 27002 are discussed in more detail later in this book.

The 2013 editions of ISO 27001 and ISO 27002 had 114 controls, while the 2022 editions contain 93 controls. Some controls have been merged to reduce overlap (56 controls reduced to 24) and 11 new controls have been added. The controls have also been reorganised, moving from a classification system with 14 distinct categories to a simpler system based around 4 key themes.

This book assumes you are new to ISO 27001/ISO 27002 and using the 2022 editions.

---

[2] For more on Annex SL, see 'A brief note on Annex SL' later in this chapter.

Introduction

Implementing an ISMS

This book is written to help you understand and use ISO 27001 and ISO 27002. It explains how to meet the requirements to implement a certified ISMS, but it does not offer guidance on the order those requirements should be implemented or how to implement an ISMS in a broad sense.

Implementing an ISMS is a significant undertaking and must be approached as a project. It must be carefully and effectively planned, appropriately resourced, and monitored to ensure that it is implemented in line with the Standard's requirements. While ISO management system standards are intentionally structured to allow you to implement their components in the order presented by the clauses, the necessities of business often require a less linear approach.

To learn how IT Governance recommends implementing an ISMS, consider *Nine Steps to Success – An ISO 27001 Implementation Overview.*[3] This comprehensive book offers detailed guidance on developing your ISMS implementation project, from inception to certification. It is suitable for organisations of any size or industry and outlines the nine steps that IT Governance considers essential to a successful implementation project.

---

[3] *https://www.itgovernancepublishing.co.uk/product/nine-steps-to-success*.

Plan-Do-Check-Act

Plan-do-check-act (PDCA) is an iterative continual improvement methodology that originated in the post-Second World War quality management movement. Although PDCA has not formally been part of ISO 27001 since the 2005 edition, it is still considered a best-practice approach, and as such you should expect to encounter it in training materials and media related to ISO 27001 and other management system standards.

The PDCA cycle is simple to apply. Before making a change, plan how it should proceed and acquire any necessary resources (plan). Once your planning is complete, make the change in accordance with the plan (do). Once the change has been implemented, monitor and evaluate its effectiveness (check), then use the information gained to make improvements (act).

Each iteration of the cycle improves your knowledge of the system, ensuring that changes proceed in a controlled manner and allowing any change that introduces a detrimental effect to be quickly identified and mitigated. Planning and monitoring should be proportionate to the change in question so the process does not become needlessly onerous.

PDCA is one of many continual improvement methodologies and the Standard does not mandate its use – only that the organisation continually improves the ISMS. If your organisation uses a different approach, it can continue to do so, provided the requirements of the Standard are met. For those organisations without an embedded improvement methodology, however, PDCA offers a simple and easy-to-understand approach.

A brief note on Annex SL

Until 2011, all ISO management system standards were developed relatively independently. Although they all share core components such as internal audit or management review, each one implemented those components slightly differently. This lack of commonality increased costs and complexity for organisations operating more than one management system, creating a barrier to adoption.

In 2011, ISO addressed the issue by introducing Annex SL: a new framework that defined how management system standards are written. It defines a common high-level clause structure and core text so that all management system standards use the same wording for shared components. This enhances compatibility and interoperability, allowing organisations that operate more than one management system to integrate core requirements like internal audit as a single, overarching process instead of implementing a separate process for each management system.

There is an occasional misconception that certification bodies audit against Annex SL. It arises because the core wording of shared components like internal audit is defined in Annex SL, but you will always be audited against the standard you are seeking certification against, not against Annex SL itself.

Shall and should

ISO management system standards use specific terms when referring to requirements and recommendations. If a clause uses the term 'shall', the requirement in that clause is mandatory if you intend to achieve accredited certification. Such clauses are the principal focus of certification and surveillance audits, and you should consider how you might demonstrate compliance with them to an auditor, particularly where the clause does not contain a requirement for documented information.

Clauses that use terms like 'should' and 'may' are recommendations and best-practice guidance and are not generally auditable. These terms are more common in guidance standards such as ISO 27002 than in 'specification' standards like ISO 27001.

CHAPTER 1: ACCREDITED CERTIFICATION

While implementing an ISO 27001-compliant ISMS provides significant benefits, the greatest commercial benefit is achieved through accredited certification. Clients and customers will not simply accept your word that your ISMS is effective and that you take information security seriously – they will expect you to prove it.

Accredited certification is overseen by national accreditation bodies (that are in turn overseen by the International Accreditation Forum (IAF)). These bodies certify the competence of organisations that offer certification against national or international standards (usually called 'certification bodies'), ensuring that their assessments are carried out in line with internationally recognised requirements.

The UK's national accreditation body is the United Kingdom Accreditation Service (UKAS), and there are equivalent bodies in most countries around the world. However, it is important to note that in most jurisdictions there is no legal requirement for a certification body to be accredited. This creates a two-tier system of certification: those issued by accredited certification bodies and those issued by unaccredited certification bodies.

Accredited certification is valuable because the certification body has been independently assessed as competent to evaluate compliance against the relevant standard. As a result, certificates issued by an accredited certification body are recognised by suppliers, partners and other accreditation bodies across the globe as a valid, independent determination of compliance.

Unaccredited certification may seem like a useful middle ground. It is often cheaper, with less intensive and fewer audits and certificates that remain valid for longer: perhaps six years, or ten. However, it is a false economy. Without independent verification of the certification body, organisations have no way to know whether the body is applying the Standard correctly or conducting effective audits of the management system.

As a result, most organisations will not consider unaccredited certificates satisfactory evidence. Often, they will simply reject them outright. They will assume (not without some justification) that an organisation that takes shortcuts in certification may also take shortcuts in the operation of the ISMS. The end result is, at best, increased scrutiny or audits that an accredited certificate would have prevented; at worst, loss of business that an accredited certificate could have secured.

The certification process

Certification is usually a two-stage process involving independent audits conducted by the certification body.

The initial audit focuses on whether you are implementing the ISMS correctly and in line with the Standard, and will examine various key requirements to ensure they are being met. Don't worry if the auditor discovers nonconformities (i.e. parts of the Standard that aren't fully or correctly implemented, usually classified as 'minor' or 'major' depending on severity) at this stage – this is common, and the auditor will use them as an opportunity to help you better understand the requirements of the Standard and how they should be applied.

After the first audit, you will have a clear idea of where you are meeting requirements and where you are falling short. You can then develop an action plan to implement any necessary changes to the fledgling ISMS in preparation for the certification audit.

The certification audit follows a similar process, in that it will examine the various constituent parts of the ISMS to ensure they comply with the Standard. The auditor will look for evidence that the ISMS is implemented, functional and operating effectively, which will likely involve reviewing evidence of internal audits, information security controls, monitoring and measurement results, objectives, etc.

The goal should be to begin the certification audit with confidence that there are no major nonconformities in the ISMS. Any minor issues noted can usually be resolved through your corrective action procedures, but any major nonconformities identified will likely result in the certification body refusing to issue certification until they are resolved to its satisfaction.

Maintaining certification

Once you have achieved certification, you then need to maintain it. Most accredited management system certificates are valid for three years, during which you will be subject to surveillance audits by the certification body.

Surveillance audits are usually conducted twice a year. Each audit examines different aspects of the management system (along with a subset of mandatory items that are included in all surveillance audits) so that the entire management system is independently reviewed by the time the certificate is due to expire. Members of top management should be present for surveillance audits, as they will be expected to be able to demonstrate knowledge of the ISMS and its objectives, adherence to the leadership requirements defined in Clause 5.1 of the Standard and overall responsibility for the system.

Minor nonconformities identified during surveillance audits are generally left for the organisation to resolve on its own, though auditors will expect that the nonconformity is resolved and closed by the next surveillance audit. Major nonconformities are usually resolved by developing and applying a corrective action plan that is agreed with the certification body.

If a management system is shown to be in conformity for extended periods (e.g. no nonconformities are identified for a whole three-year certification cycle), then the number of surveillance audits in future certification cycles may be reduced. Reducing the number of surveillance audits is entirely at the discretion of the certification body, however, and is never guaranteed.

Recertification

Towards the end of the certificate's lifespan, you will undergo a recertification audit. This will be similar to the certification audit and will examine your ISMS in detail, with additional focus on the effectiveness and performance of the system as implemented, the effectiveness of information security controls and objectives, and continual improvement. At the conclusion of the audit, the lead auditor will make a recommendation to the certification body in respect of your recertification.

Minor nonconformities identified during the recertification assessment are unlikely to affect the lead auditor's recommendation, unless they are present in large numbers or are indicative of a more significant problem. If any major nonconformities are identified, however, it is likely that the lead auditor will not recommend that your certification is renewed until they are resolved.

If this occurs, you will need to agree a corrective action plan with the certification body. This will describe how you will resolve the nonconformity and set a time frame within which another recertification audit must be conducted. If the nonconformity is not resolved, or the second recertification audit reveals further major nonconformities, then your certification will almost certainly be suspended or revoked.

The final decision always rests with the certification body. Most certification bodies permit the organisation to dispute the findings of an audit, but you should be very sure of your ground before making a complaint.

CHAPTER 2: TERMS AND DEFINITIONS

ISO 27000:2018 defines key terms and definitions that are used across the ISO 27000 series of standards.[4] You should read and understand these definitions before working your way through ISO 27001 and ISO 27002. Some of the most important ones are below:

- **Attack** – attempt to destroy, expose, alter, disable, steal or gain unauthorized access to or make unauthorized use of an asset.
- **Audit** – systematic, independent and documented process for obtaining audit evidence and evaluating it objectively to determine the extent to which the audit criteria are fulfilled.
- **Availability** – property of being accessible and usable on demand by an authorized entity.
- **Confidentiality** – property that information is not made available or disclosed to unauthorized individuals, entities, or processes.
- **Control** – measure that is modifying risk.
- **Documented information** – information required to be controlled and maintained by an organization and the medium on which it is contained.
- **Information security** – preservation of confidentiality, integrity and availability of information.

---

[4] ISO 27000:2018, Clause 3.

- **Integrity** – property of accuracy and completeness.
- **Interested party** – person or organization that can affect, be affected by, or perceive itself to be affected by a decision or activity.
- **Management system** – set of interrelated or interacting elements of an organization to establish policies and objectives and processes to achieve those objectives.
- **Nonconformity** – non-fulfilment of a requirement.
- **Objective** – result to be achieved.
- **Risk** – effect of uncertainty on objectives.
- **Risk assessment** – overall process of risk identification, risk analysis and risk evaluation.
- **Threat** – potential cause of an unwanted incident, which can result in harm to a system or organization.
- **Vulnerability** – weakness of an asset or control that can be exploited by one or more threats.

Additionally, ISO 55000:2014 *Asset management — Overview, principles and terminology* defines an asset as an *"item, thing or entity that has actual or potential value to an organisation"*.[5]

---

[5] ISO 55000:2014, Clause 3.2.1.

CHAPTER 3: ISO 27001 REQUIREMENTS

Like all ISO standards aligned to Annex SL, the first three clauses define the scope of the standard, the normative references and the terms and definitions used throughout.

ISO 27001 has only one normative reference – ISO 27000, from which the terms and definitions are also taken. Those terms and definitions (only) can be viewed freely online through the preview function of ISO's online browsing platform.[6]

4 – Context of the organisation

Clause 4 is concerned with identifying the key operational context that your organisation operates within to better inform the scope and function of the ISMS. The organisation is expected to determine internal and external issues that are relevant to its purpose, and that could affect its ability to achieve the intended outcomes of the ISMS.

It must also identify interested parties that are relevant to the ISMS and their requirements, and define which of those requirements will be addressed through the ISMS. Once this is done, the organisation must use this information to define the scope of the ISMS.

---

[6] To view the definitions through ISO's online browsing platform, navigate to *https://www.iso.org/standard/73906.html*.

Internal and external issues

A common approach to determining internal and external issues is a 'PESTLE' analysis. This method focuses on identifying the political, economic, social, technological, legal and environmental issues relevant to the organisation through research and discussion. The organisation should collate information for each category, paying particular attention to legal requirements that could influence the ISMS.

External issues might include the following:

- Political issues in the jurisdictions that you operate in such as the formation of new regulators or the development of new information security or privacy legislation.
- Economic factors such as trends that drive a particular type of data processing, the potential impact of fines and penalties, or any external economic issue that could affect the organisation's ability to procure appropriate equipment, personnel and controls.
- Social issues. This category could include anything from the broader social consensus around the types of data that you hold or the processing you perform, the impact of a particular type of data breach, or changes to how the use of data is perceived by members of the public.
- Technical issues. Technology is constantly changing and evolving, resulting in encryption methods that become unviable due to inherent vulnerabilities or

increased computing power, new malware and newly identified vulnerabilities, or key software or hardware becoming obsolete or unsupported.

- Legal issues. This could include privacy and information security laws that are already in force or that are anticipated, contractual requirements imposed by customers, or the threat of enforcement action by regulators.
- Environmental issues, which could range from the organisation's overall carbon footprint to concerns around disposal of IT hardware, use of recyclable materials, and so on.

Internal issues are likely to include things like the working environment, personnel (requirements, training and skills), resources, hardware and equipment, the premises you operate out of and the effects of the organisation's internal culture and capabilities. The PESTLE method is less suitable for internal issues, so you might opt for a simple list or very broad categories such as positive and negative.

Although they are harder to identify, internal issues often have the most direct effect on the functioning of a management system because they tend to relate to *how* you do things rather than *what* must be done. Accounting for them is a key part of successful implementation planning.

Interested parties

Interested parties (or stakeholders, to use an equivalent term) will depend heavily on the nature of your organisation, but essentially include anyone 'relevant to the

ISMS'. Key interested parties are likely to include regulators and enforcement bodies, certification bodies, the organisation's personnel (including contractors) and partners, clients and customers, suppliers and service providers, and even the organisation's neighbours (e.g. if it shares an office building). The outcome of the exercise you use to identify the context of the organisation will usually provide pointers as to who your interested parties might be.

Once you have identified your interested parties, you can determine their requirements and which are relevant to the ISMS. Some of these will be readily apparent – regulators will require that you comply with relevant legislation and legal requirements, customers and clients will require that you protect their data and uphold your contractual obligations, and so on. In less obvious cases, you may need to conduct research to identify requirements, or it may be necessary to contact the party directly to ask.

As you identify requirements, you will find that some need to be addressed through the ISMS. The Standard explicitly mandates you to determine the requirements that will be addressed through the ISMS, so you should take note of any that fall into this category.

There is no requirement to document the outcome of the exercises you conduct to identify the context of the organisation and the requirements of interested parties. Despite this, you may find it beneficial to do so. Keeping a record helps you track how these things change over time and can inform future changes to the ISMS. If you do not keep records, you should consider how you might demonstrate compliance with these requirements to an auditor – you might have a knowledgeable member of top management explain them verbally, for example.

Determining the scope of the ISMS

The next part of the Standard requires that you define the scope of the ISMS – i.e. what parts of the organisation the management system will apply to. For smaller organisations, the scope will usually encompass the entire organisation. Larger organisations may prefer to limit the scope of the ISMS to specific business functions or sites.

When defining the scope, you should account for relevant aspects of the context of the organisation and the requirements of interested parties (for example, if an interested party requires that a certain part of your organisation is protected by your ISMS, it would not be acceptable to exclude that part of the organisation from the scope), and the interfaces between the activities your organisation performs and those that are performed by other organisations.

The scope should describe the services, functions and locations (etc.) within the purview of the ISMS, along with any interdependencies between your systems and those of other organisations to the extent they remain under your control. The scope can only comprise functions within the management authority of your organisation; outsourced processes can be included, but the organisations that perform those processes (and other external suppliers) are not under your authority and therefore cannot be part of your scope.

The scope statement should clearly define the logical (i.e. networks and systems) and physical boundaries of the

ISMS. Depending on the nature of the organisation and the products or services it provides, the scope may include the whole organisation or only parts of the organisation. An international organisation that operates in five countries, for example, may choose to implement an ISMS to satisfy regulatory requirements in one country, but determine that it is not financially viable to do so in the other four. In such a case, the scope would be restricted to the sites and networks/systems in that one country.

The scope statement must be maintained as documented information. You may also find it necessary to provide the scope statement to interested parties on occasion, so you should ensure it is clearly written and in an accessible format.

5 – Leadership

Leadership is essential for the success of any management system, yet management is not the same thing as leadership. An influential professor at Harvard Business School, John P. Kotter, once said: *"Management is about coping with complexity […]. Leadership, by contrast, is about coping with change."*[7] Good leaders inspire and encourage those around them – they set the direction for an organisation and help those responsible to achieve that direction. It is in this sense that ISO 27001 uses the term.

Top management must understand the risks associated with the processing and storage of information to fully

---

[7] John P. Kotter, "What Leaders Really Do", *Harvard Business Review*, 2001, *https://hbr.org/2001/12/what-leaders-really-do*.

understand the value of a formal system dedicated to managing it. They must promote and encourage the application of that system across the whole organisation and be seen to comply with it themselves. An ISMS that is not supported by the organisation's top management will, in most cases, ultimately fail.

This does not mean that top management must become information security or IT experts to implement a successful ISMS. Technical and project management tasks can be delegated to suitable personnel just as with any other major business project. Instead, top management must help the organisation adapt to the changes and incorporate the requirements of the ISMS into day-to-day operations.

Leadership and commitment

Clause 5.1 places a formal obligation on top management to demonstrate leadership in respect of the ISMS. They must:

- Establish policies and objectives;
- Ensure that the ISMS is integrated into the organisation's processes;
- Provide appropriate resources;
- Communicate the importance of effective information security and of conforming to the ISMS' requirements;
- Ensure that the ISMS achieves its intended outcomes;
- Promote continual improvement; and
- Direct and support management and personnel to contribute to the effectiveness of the ISMS.

Some of these things will happen naturally if the ISMS implementation project is effectively planned and appropriately budgeted – you would expect top management to support management and personnel in contributing to the effectiveness of the ISMS, for example, and resources will necessarily be required for any significant project. Promoting continual improvement and communicating the importance of information security and the ISMS itself can be achieved through periodic briefings, email communications or other methods.

The requirement to ensure that the ISMS achieves its intended outcomes highlights that top management are ultimately accountable for the performance of the ISMS. Though they will no doubt delegate the day-to-day operation and maintenance of the ISMS to others, they should understand that overall responsibility for the ISMS remains theirs.

Policy

The information security policy is one of the most important documents in the ISMS. Top management must establish the policy and ensure it meets the requirements of the Standard: it must be appropriate to the organisation's purpose, include information security objectives or provide a framework for setting them, and include commitments to satisfy applicable information security requirements and to continually improve the ISMS.

As a rule of thumb, it is better for the policy to provide a framework for setting information security objectives rather than to include the objectives themselves. The core policy language is unlikely to change significantly over time, while objectives may need to be updated or replaced as the ISMS evolves. If the policy provides a framework for those objectives (who will define them, how they will be monitored, when they will be reviewed, etc.), there is no need to update and reissue the policy each time an individual objective changes.

As a top-level policy, the information security policy will necessarily be quite broad. It should define the organisation's approach in a general sense, while pointing to other subject-specific policies and procedures that contain the details. It should also be written in plain language, with minimal jargon and technical terminology to make it accessible to those without an IT or information security background.

The policy must be available as documented information, and it must be communicated both within the organisation and to relevant interested parties. You could communicate it internally through emails, information security awareness briefings and in-house training sessions, and retain a PDF or similarly protected version to issue to interested parties as required.

Organisational roles, responsibilities and authorities

Top management are also expected to ensure that responsibilities for information security are assigned and communicated. In particular, they must assign responsibility and authority for ensuring that the ISMS conforms to the requirements of the Standard and for reporting on the performance of the ISMS to top management. In many small and medium-sized enterprises, the same person may be responsible for both.

It should be noted that the Standard explicitly uses the term 'responsibility and authority'. Those responsible for the ISMS need an appropriate level of authority to effectively perform their role – without it, the implementation process will be impaired and the ongoing effectiveness of the ISMS may be reduced.

One often misunderstood aspect of this requirement is that the person with overall responsibility for the day-to-day management of the ISMS need not be an IT expert. They should have a broad understanding of information security as a subject and be conscious of the current threat landscape, but they do not need to understand computer code or the technical necessities of network or server administration, software development, and so on.

Your IT personnel will need the knowledge and skills to help assess IT-related information security risks and implement technical security controls, but the person with overall responsibility for the ISMS is usually better served by programme and project management skills and a strong understanding of ISO management systems.

6 – Planning

This part of the Standard is focused on planning for and addressing risks and opportunities that may affect the ISMS, and on assessing and treating information security risks. Both aspects are an essential part of an effective ISMS.

Actions to address risks and opportunities

The inputs for this clause are the internal and external issues and the requirements of interested parties that you identified under Clause 4 – Context of the organisation. These must be evaluated to identify risks and opportunities that need to be addressed to ensure the ISMS achieves its intended outcomes, prevent or reduce undesired effects, and achieve continual improvement. It is important to note that Clause 6.1.1 targets risks and opportunities that can affect the ISMS, not those that could affect information security.

The organisation is expected to plan actions to address the risks and opportunities that arise from the context of the organisation, integrate those actions into ISMS processes, and evaluate their effectiveness. There is no requirement to maintain documented information on the risks you identify under 6.1.1 or the process you use to do so.

Despite this, it would be beneficial to keep some records of the process and its outcomes. Doing so will help you repeat the process consistently as the organisation's context changes, and practicality suggests that you will need to document some actions to properly evaluate them, particularly if their effectiveness can only be measured over long periods.

Information security risk assessment

This clause, and the one that follows it, are arguably two of the most important in the Standard. The information security risk assessment and treatment processes are fundamental to the success of the ISMS and should be given careful consideration. You must be aware of risks before you can treat them, and you must be able to effectively and consistently evaluate the level of risk to determine which risks need to be treated and to what extent.

The Standard expects you to *"define and apply"* an information security risk assessment process. This process must establish and maintain risk acceptance criteria and criteria for performing information security risk assessments, and must ensure that those assessments produce *"consistent, valid and comparable results"*.[8]

Assessing risk is a process of evaluating the likelihood and potential impact of a risk occurring and deciding what to do based on the outcome. The criteria you are expected to establish are the scales against which you will judge likelihood and impact – you can use quantitative or qualitative scales, or a combination of both – and the level of risk you are prepared to tolerate.

Regardless of which method you use, there will be a threshold beneath which you consider risks to be acceptable – that is, the likelihood or impact is so low as to render the risk negligible or the cost of treating it significantly disproportionate. This threshold is your risk acceptance criteria (or 'risk appetite'), and it should be clearly defined in your risk assessment methodology.

For example, if you use five-point scales for likelihood and impact and multiply the two values to reach a final score, you will end up with a grid like this:

---

[8] ISO 27001:2022, Clause 6.1.2.

Table 1: Five-Point Scale for Likelihood

5	10	15	20	25
4	8	12	16	20
3	6	9	12	15
2	4	6	8	10
1	2	3	4	5

(Impact on vertical axis; Likelihood on horizontal axis)

Likelihood

If you were to set your acceptance criteria as anything below four, you could represent that on the grid like this:

Table 2: Acceptance Criteria

5	10	15	20	25
4	8	12	16	20
3	6	9	12	15
2	4	6	8	10
1	2	3	4	5

(Impact on vertical axis; Likelihood on horizontal axis)

Likelihood

Any risk that falls within the green cells would be considered acceptable. Any risk that falls outside the green cells would require treatment.

Even the most detailed risk assessment methodology will occasionally produce outliers that exceed the acceptance criteria on paper, yet do not present a significant real-world risk. For example, we would probably judge the impact of a major earthquake on a UK-based organisation at five (because UK buildings aren't traditionally made earthquake-resistant) and the likelihood at one (because major tectonic events in the UK are incredibly rare), for a final score of five. This exceeds our risk acceptance criteria (anything below 4), so in theory, we should do something to mitigate it – yet few UK organisations would consider it justified to do so.

Outlier results are inevitable, so your risk assessment methodology should set out what you will do when you encounter them. You might define a set of rules that apply to risks with the lowest possible likelihood or impact scores, or approach each outlier on a case-by-case basis and simply define the questions you will ask to determine if the risk can be safely tolerated.

The Standard expects you to identify risks *"associated with the loss of confidentiality, integrity and availability"* to information in scope of the ISMS.[9] Confidentiality, integrity and availability are sometimes referred to as the 'CIA' of information security, and each risk you identify should be assessed in terms of these three properties.

---

[9] ISO 27001:2022, Clause 6.1.2.

When we think of confidentiality risks, we often think of dedicated criminal hackers trying to access databases or servers with thousands or millions of records. However, breaches of confidentiality can also include common mistakes like accidentally emailing a file containing personal information to the wrong person or an employee reading records they should not have access to.

Risks to integrity could range from corruption or damage to entire datasets resulting from major technical failure, to entering the wrong address when updating a customer record. Risks to availability could include loss of access to records due to a ransomware attack, forgetting the password needed to access protected records or deleting records that should be retained. If a given risk has a very wide-ranging effect, it may be beneficial to split that risk into multiple parts so its components can be examined in more detail.

When assessing risk, remember that people are naturally biased towards the risks that directly affect them. A vulnerability that shuts down access to the organisation's spreadsheet software could be a big deal for the finance team but less so for the customer service team, and each team would score the impact differently. To minimise this, risk assessment teams should be multidisciplinary and comprise personnel from all areas of the business. You can also appoint an independent moderator to oversee the process and ensure that risks are judged consistently across the organisation.

Your risk assessment process must be applied consistently to produce comparable results. This means that everyone involved should understand what each level of the scales means and the level of risk the organisation is prepared to tolerate, how scores are calculated or results arrived at, and how to record the results. Internal audits of the process should sample several assessments to evaluate whether scores are properly applied, whether the actions recommended by each assessment are appropriate and whether outlier results are being properly managed.

Assets, threats and vulnerabilities

Information security risks are usually expressed in terms of assets, threats and vulnerabilities.

An asset is anything that has value to the organisation: the information you hold, the server hardware it is stored on, the building the server is in, the staff who operate it, and so on. Assets are often classified as primary or supporting: the information you hold is a primary asset, while the medium it is stored on is a supporting asset.

Primary assets often have multiple supporting assets: for example, a web application (supporting) can hold multiple information assets (primary), and the application might access that information from a database (supporting), which itself runs on server hardware (supporting). To perform information security risk assessments, you must have an inventory of all the assets – primary and supporting – in the organisation.

You may recall that ISO 27000 defines a threat as a *"potential cause of an unwanted incident, which can result in harm to a system or organization"*.[10] Threats can be

---

[10] ISO 27000:2018, Clause 3.74.

deliberate, accidental or environmental depending on their source, and can range from deliberate hacking attempts to acts of human error or 'acts of God' like earthquakes or tornados.

A vulnerability is defined as a *"weakness of an asset or control that can be exploited by one or more threats"*.[11] Such weaknesses can take many forms and are heavily dependent on the asset or control in question: a web application has very different weaknesses to an office building, for example.

To identify information security risks, you must first identify your assets. You can then review each asset to identify any vulnerabilities that might affect it and any threats that might exploit those vulnerabilities. You should involve asset owners in this activity, as they are likely to have the best understanding of the vulnerabilities that might be present and can provide insight that you can use to identify risks you may not be aware of.

Once you have identified your risks, you must analyse their likelihood and potential impact using the criteria you developed in Clause 6 to determine a level of risk, then evaluate that level of risk against your risk acceptance criteria. The results allow you to prioritise risk treatments, with greater risks afforded greater urgency.

The Standard also expects you to identify an owner for each risk. 'Owner' in this context means the person(s) responsible for the asset, operation or function with which

---

[11] ISO 27000:2018, Clause 3.77.

the risk is associated, or the person responsible for managing the risk (whichever is more appropriate).

Risk owners will be responsible for approving risk treatments (where the risk falls outside your acceptance criteria) and for accepting and monitoring any residual risk that remains after treatment.

You must retain documented information on the results of the information security risk assessment process. At a minimum, this should include the assessments themselves and a record showing risk owners and the actions taken to mitigate risks.

Information security risk treatment

You must develop a documented process that defines how you will treat the risks you have identified and evaluated. Risk treatment options are often expressed as 'the four Ts': tolerate, treat, transfer and terminate:

1. Tolerate means simply accepting the risk with no further action and would be applied to anything that falls within your acceptance criteria, as well as to any unusual outliers as mentioned earlier. This is also referred to as accepting or retaining a risk.

2. Treat means to take action to reduce either the likelihood or impact (or both) so that, once the treatment is applied and confirmed to be working, the risk score falls within your acceptance criteria. This is also referred to as modifying a risk.

3. Transfer means to pass the risk to someone else, for example by outsourcing the activity to a third party

that can better manage the risk, or by purchasing insurance to mitigate the impact. Transferring a risk does not mean it no longer exists, and a transferred risk should still be monitored and re-evaluated to ensure that the transfer measures remain appropriate. This is also referred to as sharing a risk.

4. Terminate means to stop performing the activity that results in the risk. If storing certain types of sensitive data gives rise to an unacceptable risk, you might terminate that risk by not collecting that data in the first place. This is also referred to as avoiding a risk.

If it is necessary to treat a risk, the Standard expects you to determine the controls necessary to do so. Controls are the mitigating actions that you apply to reduce the risk level, such as applying encryption, implementing firewalls, and so on.

You can select controls from any source or develop your own. Annex A of ISO 27001 contains a list of controls (ISO 27002 describes them in more detail) and should be your initial source, as you are expected to consider all of them or justify their absence when implementing your ISMS.

You can also use controls from any other information security framework, such as NIST SP 800-53 or the Payment Card Industry Data Security Standard (PCI DSS). Whatever externally sourced controls you select or develop, you must compare them to the controls in Annex A to verify that no necessary controls (i.e. those related to the risks you have identified) have been omitted.

All this information must be gathered in a Statement of Applicability (SoA). The SoA must list all the controls in Annex A, together with justifications for their inclusion or exclusion and the status of their implementation. If you develop additional controls or use controls from other frameworks, they must also be listed, along with the justification for their inclusion and their implementation status.

The SoA is one of the most important documents in your ISMS, and it must be both comprehensive and carefully maintained. It should be treated as documented information and therefore be subject to version control, and it should be periodically reviewed to ensure it remains up to date.

The SoA will be a key focus during certification and surveillance audits by your chosen certification body, and the version of the SoA that was current during your certification audit will usually be listed on your ISO 27001 certificate of compliance. You may be called upon to provide the SoA to interested parties to demonstrate the degree of security that you have implemented, so it is important that it is legible and complete. Due to the amount of information the SoA must contain and the need for accessibility, they are commonly developed in spreadsheet software – though there is nothing preventing you from exploring alternative formats.

With your risks identified and evaluated and your controls selected, the Standard requires that you develop a risk treatment plan. This should lay out the actions, responsibilities and priorities to implement the controls and evaluate their outcomes. Risk owners must approve their respective actions and the controls themselves, along with any residual risk that remains once a given risk has been treated.

The Standard requires that you retain documented information about the risk treatment process. Along with the process, the SoA and the risk treatment plan should also be treated as documented information (even though the Standard does not explicitly call for it in Clause 6.1.3). Most auditors will consider these documents 'necessary for the effectiveness of the ISMS' in line with Clause 7.5.1.b, which we will look at later.

Information security objectives

This part of the Standard requires the organisation to define information security objectives. These must be consistent with the information security policy, be measurable (where practicable), take into account the results of information security risk assessments and treatments, be monitored, and be communicated throughout the organisation. The objectives must be available as documented information, and they must be updated as appropriate (i.e. when they are revised or replaced).

It is important to understand that these objectives should relate to information security, not to the ISMS itself. A common format for such objectives is 'SMART', in which objectives should be specific, measurable, achievable, realistic and time-bound – though you may use any format that meets the requirements.

The Standard also expects you to plan how to achieve these objectives, and determine what must be done, who is responsible, what resources are required, when they will be completed and how they will be evaluated. You do not have to maintain documented information on this planning or of any subsequent evaluation, but you may consider keeping some records (though not necessarily subject to the requirements for documented information) to demonstrate compliance with these requirements to an auditor.

Planning of changes

This clause requires the organisation to carry out any changes to the ISMS *"in a planned manner"*.[12] There is no requirement for a defined procedure or for documented information to be retained as evidence.

This very broad requirement allows considerable leeway in how you interpret it. If you already have a change management process, you could adapt it to encompass the ISMS. If you do not have a formal change management process, this is a good prompt to create one (particularly for larger organisations where the risk associated with unplanned changes is naturally higher).

Smaller organisations or those that decide no formal process is necessary can 'get by' with ad hoc planning – though you should consider how you might demonstrate compliance with the requirement to an auditor.

7 – Support

This part of the Standard defines requirements for support of the ISMS, both during implementation and while

---

[12] ISO 27001:2022, Clause 6.3.

maintaining it. It covers resources, competence, awareness, communication and documented information.

Resources

The organisation is expected to provide the resources needed for *"the establishment, implementation, maintenance and continual improvement"* of the ISMS.[13] The specific resources you will need will vary from organisation to organisation and across the various lifecycle stages of the ISMS, but could include equipment and infrastructure, software and systems, personnel and training, and external services such as penetration testing.

Resources are a key factor to consider when planning to implement your ISMS, but you should also plan carefully for the resources needed to maintain it. You will need to consider replacement equipment, software licences, training costs and similar expenses, and – perhaps most important – you will need to ensure that personnel affected by the ISMS have the time they need to carry out ISMS-related tasks.

Competence

This four-part sub-clause requires the organisation to determine the necessary level of competence for personnel who affect information security performance; ensure that the relevant personnel meet that level through education, training or experience; take action to ensure personnel acquire that competence where the level is not already met

---

[13] ISO 27001:2022, Clause 7.1.

(e.g. through training); and evaluate those actions to determine their effectiveness.

Most organisations will already operate a training plan of one sort or another, so you will likely need to adapt it to meet the requirements of the Standard. You will need to identify all the roles in the organisation that can reasonably affect information security performance, then determine the necessary competence levels for each one. Once this is done, you can design a training regime to account for any current gaps. You may also want to consider periodic refresher training for key personnel.

The organisation must maintain documented information as evidence of competence. Most organisations approach this by keeping a competence record that contains the expected levels for all relevant personnel, the actions taken and the results of evaluations (e.g. in a spreadsheet).

Awareness

This clause requires the organisation to ensure that persons who work under its control are aware of the information security policy, their contribution to the effectiveness of the ISMS, and what could happen if they do not conform to its requirements.

For any management system to effectively function, those working under it must be aware of core policies and procedures that underpin the system and how their role is affected by relevant requirements. Ensuring awareness of the information security policy might be as simple as making it available on an internal network and emailing all staff to ask them to read it, while the other requirements might be addressed by conducting staff awareness meetings or 'town hall' discussions.

You may also need to update your organisation's disciplinary policy to define what will happen in cases of repeated or wilful failure to adhere to the ISMS or its requirements. Some organisations will consider it necessary to develop specific offences, while others may be content to group such behaviour under more general misconduct clauses – how you go about this is up to you. All the Standard requires is that the consequences of not adhering to requirements are defined.

There is some overlap between this clause and control 6.3 in Annex A (Information security awareness, education and training), and many organisations opt to address both requirements through the same training programme.

Communication

There will naturally be a need for internal and external communications related to the ISMS throughout its lifetime, and this clause defines requirements for those communications. This is a very broad clause, requiring only that the organisation defines who, when and how to communicate, and on what subjects.

Over the life of the ISMS, you will likely need to communicate about changes across the business that result from the ISMS, new threats and vulnerabilities, changes to key processes and controls, and other related aspects. You may also need to communicate with regulators and other interested parties (e.g. if a notifiable data breach occurs). There should be a clear chain of responsibility and approval for communications of different types, particularly those addressed to parties outside the organisation.

Documented information

Throughout the Standard, you will find references to 'documented information'. This means that the documents the Standard is asking for are subject to specific requirements. Clause 7.5 defines those requirements, and how they are met has ramifications for the whole ISMS.

7.5a states that the ISMS must contain documented information required by the Standard, while 7.5b requires that the ISMS include documented information *"determined by the organization as being necessary for the effectiveness"* of the management system. The former case is relatively self-explanatory – many clauses contain a requirement to maintain documented information, and all of them must be complied with.

In the latter case, it's up to your organisation to decide what additional documentation should be treated as documented information, but it should include core ISMS documents like the SoA and risk treatment plan.

The next part says that when you create documented information, you must ensure appropriate identification and description, format, and review and approval for suitability and adequacy. Each item of documented information should have a unique identifier and an appropriate title; for electronic documents, this is usually in the file name and the document header or footer (e.g. ISMS_DOC_001 Internal Audit Procedure).

Review and approval should involve a mechanism that defines how often a document is reviewed and who is responsible for approving it to confirm that it is still suitable. Larger organisations often have a defined review procedure that covers all documented information and defines the necessary review periods and responsibilities; smaller organisations might opt to define review periods and the roles responsible for review and approval in the document itself.

Format can be anything the organisation considers suitable for the information the document contains. Spreadsheets will naturally be more suitable for storing large amounts of information, while Word documents will probably lend themselves to procedures and reports, but if you find other formats more appropriate (e.g. a computer application or database), you can use them.

The last section of this clause defines requirements for control of documented information. First, it must be available and suitable for use when needed, and it must be adequately protected against loss of confidentiality or integrity, improper use, and other risks that might render it unusable or ineffective.

To ensure effective control, you must also address the distribution, access, retrieval and use, storage and preservation, control of changes, and retention and disposition of your documented information. How you choose to meet the control requirements will necessarily affect the operation of the entire ISMS, so you should develop a document control procedure (that will itself be documented information) that sets out how you will address each requirement.

The aphorism 'less is more' is highly relevant here – you don't need to leap straight to expensive document control software to meet these requirements. You could control changes and manage retention by recording version numbers and retention periods in a spreadsheet, and address access and retrieval by making documents available through a company intranet, or simply by placing printed copies in folders at the point of use and periodically checking them to make sure they are up to date. You can also use more commonly available software such as Microsoft SharePoint instead of costly bespoke solutions.

Finally, you are also expected to identify and control *"documented information of external origin"* that you have determined necessary for the planning and operation of the ISMS.[14] This might include standards and industry guidance documents, service level agreements, or other documents that feed into ISMS planning or operational requirements. These documents should be subject to the control requirements of Clause 7.5.3.

8 – Operational planning and control

Clause 8 is focused on implementing core ISMS processes in your organisation's workflow and the overall operation of the ISMS as a system.

Clause 6 of the Standard asks that you identify risks and opportunities that can affect the operation of the ISMS and plan actions to address them. Clause 8.1 requires that you *"plan, implement and control the processes needed to meet*

---

[14] ISO 27001:2022, Clause 7.5.3.

requirements, and to implement the actions determined in Clause 6".[15] You will need to develop criteria for these processes (i.e. define the principles that will guide their development and implementation, and how you will measure performance and effectiveness) and ensure they are controlled in line with that criteria.

You must retain documented information *"to the extent necessary"* to have confidence that these processes are being carried out as planned. What is 'necessary' will differ depending on the organisation, but might include process records or outputs, logs or project plans.

8.1 also asks that you control planned changes, review the consequences of unintended changes and act to mitigate any adverse effects that such changes may produce. As with Clause 6, there is no requirement for a formal change procedure or documented information. This means you can meet this requirement in different ways, formal or informal, provided you can demonstrate it to an auditor – though a formal procedure is generally considered best practice.

The final part of 8.1 requires that you control any externally provided processes, products or services that are relevant to the ISMS. Most organisations use some kind of outsourced process or service to support the business in some form, but the defining factor here is whether they are relevant to the ISMS – if they store data, or if their use impacts the organisation's information security in some way.

---

[15] ISO 27001:2022, Clause 8.1.

The wording does not specify how much control is required or what form that control should take. In many cases, the degree of control you can exercise over an externally provided process, product or service is necessarily limited. Amazon is not going to adapt its Cloud security measures to the whims of individual customers – you either accept its terms and the security measures it provides, or you don't use the service.

In such cases, you should carefully evaluate the information security implications of the service and its security measures, then develop and apply controls to those aspects that are within your purview. To use our earlier example, you have little choice but to accept Amazon's security measures if you intend to use its·Cloud services, but you can implement controls to manage who can access the service, what data is stored within it, how and where that data is backed up, and plug any holes in your organisation's security that are necessary for the service to operate.

8.2 and 8.3 require you to implement the information security risk assessment and risk treatment processes you developed back in Clause 6. Risk assessment must be performed *"at planned intervals and whenever significant changes are proposed or occur"* using the criteria developed in 6.1.2.

'Planned intervals' leaves it entirely up to you how often you perform risk assessments, but most organisations do so at least annually. Alongside significant changes, the criteria you developed should also define other scenarios that trigger risk assessment such as suffering a data breach, identifying a new vulnerability that could affect the organisation's systems, or the introduction of a new data security regulation.

The risk treatment plan you developed for Clause 6 must also be implemented. This is by nature an ongoing process – risks change over time and as the ISMS evolves, you will need to implement new controls and retire or modify existing ones. Treatments should be monitored as necessary to ensure they are effective and achieve their intended goals.

You must retain documented information on the results of information security risk assessments and risk treatments. What that information looks like will depend on your organisation, but might include records of actions taken to treat risks and of any post-treatment evaluations, risk assessment process outputs or corrective actions.

9 – Performance evaluation

Clause 9 of the Standard is focused on performance evaluation and governance. The adage 'you can't improve what you don't measure' is just as applicable to management systems as it is to general business, and the requirements of this clause are usually considered 'mandatory items' that certification bodies will examine in every surveillance audit (unlike other aspects of the ISMS, which tend to be sampled to ensure full coverage over the three-year recertification cycle rather than at every surveillance audit).

Monitoring and measurement

Clause 9 is split into three main requirements, each of which is mandatory in a certified ISMS. 9.1 – monitoring, measurement and evaluation – obligates the organisation to determine what aspects of the ISMS need to be monitored and measured; how, when and who will undertake the measurements; and when the results will be analysed and evaluated and who is responsible for doing so.

While it is up to the organisation to decide what needs to be monitored and measured, 9.1a is clear that information security processes and controls must be considered as part of that process. You should take a risk-based approach to this requirement, prioritising high-risk or critical processes and controls over lower-risk ones.

The organisation must also define the methods it will use to monitor, measure, analyse and evaluate. This provides considerable freedom to determine methods that suit the organisation, and the nature of an ISMS means that multiple methods will invariably be needed – after all, a method suitable for monitoring a process that is carried out by hand will probably not be suitable for monitoring a hardware-based security control.

Whatever methods you decide to use, the Standard says that they should provide comparable and reproducible results. This is best achieved through a defined procedure (or set of procedures) for all but the smallest organisations, and although the Standard only requires documented information as evidence of the *results* of monitoring and measurement, it can be argued that 7.5b (documented information necessary for the effectiveness of the ISMS) applies. Monitoring and measurement are certainly necessary for an effective ISMS, and poorly defined or uncontrolled procedures are unlikely to provide consistent results.

The organisation must define the frequency of monitoring and measurement, when the results will be analysed and evaluated, and who is responsible for performing the monitoring and the eventual analysis. As with deciding what to measure, defining the frequency of monitoring and subsequent analysis should be risk-based, with higher-risk processes and controls subject to more frequent monitoring or measurement. In some cases, the frequency of monitoring might be constrained by the software or system responsible, for example if using a security incident and event management (SIEM) system.

The frequency of analysis and evaluation should also be risk-based. However, it is important to recognise that analysis and evaluation are not the same thing. Analysis is objective – you study the data collected to determine if there are patterns or trends that suggest a potential outcome. Evaluation is subjective – you review the analysed data and make judgements about whether the issues highlighted by the data require action. Some automated monitoring systems, for example, might 'analyse' the data they collect to highlight risks or vulnerabilities, but a person still needs to evaluate the output of that system to determine if the issues it brings to your attention are valid and decide what (if anything) needs to be done about them.

Evaluation should never be too decoupled from data collection and analysis. If you monitor a process daily, collate the results weekly and analyse them for trends at the end of each calendar month, but only evaluate what those trends mean in December of each year, it may be too late to respond to any issues that data shows.

The final sentence of 9.1 states: *"The organization shall evaluate the information security performance and the effectiveness of the information security management system."* This makes clear the purpose of the monitoring, and links to later requirements obligating the organisation to continually improve the ISMS.

Internal audit

Clause 9.2 provides requirements for internal audit. Like monitoring and measurement, internal audits are essential to ensure effective operation and maintenance of the ISMS. Like certification audits, internal audits examine the component parts of the ISMS to verify that they meet the requirements of the Standard and any other ISMS requirements the organisation has imposed upon itself.

ISO 27000 defines an audit as a *"systematic, independent and documented process for obtaining audit evidence and evaluating it objectively to determine the extent to which the audit criteria are fulfilled"*.[16] Although 9.2 does not explicitly require that the audit process is treated as documented information, the definition implies that it should be – and like the monitoring and measurement process, the audit process is certainly 'necessary for the effectiveness of the ISMS' and therefore falls under the remit of Clause 7.5b.

Audits are conducted on a sampling basis. For example, if auditing Clause 7.5.3 on control of documented information, the auditor is not expected to check every

---

[16] ISO 27000:2018, Clause 3.3.

single item of documented information within the organisation. Instead, the auditor should select a representative sample (e.g. two documents from each relevant business area) and check those.

9.2.1 requires the organisation to conduct internal audits at planned intervals to gain information about whether the ISMS conforms to the Standard, whether it conforms to the organisation's own requirements for the ISMS, and whether it is effectively implemented and maintained. The organisation's own requirements might stem from the requirements of interested parties that it opts to address through the ISMS, or from requirements the organisation has identified as necessary but that are not addressed in the Standard.

9.2.2 requires the organisation to develop an audit programme. The programme must be planned, established, implemented and maintained, and must define the frequency of audits, the methods used to audit, planning and reporting requirements, and the persons responsible for developing the programme and carrying it out (which may not necessarily be the same).

The internal audit programme should cover all the requirements for the ISMS (i.e. each clause of the Standard and any additional requirements). There are two common approaches to this: a programme that covers everything over a calendar or financial year, and a programme that covers everything over the three-year recertification cycle. The former is more effective but also more resource intensive, and it is up to the organisation to decide what length of audit programme is most suitable.

When developing your audit programme, the Standard requires that you consider the *"importance of the processes concerned and the results of previous audits".*[17] This is an explicitly risk-based approach – the more critical the process, the more frequently it should be audited to ensure it is working as intended. Similarly, if previous audits indicate a recurring problem with a process or control, that process or control should be audited more frequently until the problem is resolved, at which point the audit frequency can be reduced.

9.2.2 goes on to say that the organisation must define audit criteria and scope for each audit, ensure that auditors are objective and impartial, and ensure that audit results are reported to management. Your audit process should define the reporting requirements and how the audit programme is developed. Internal auditors should then reference the relevant scope and criteria in their audit reports.

Impartiality and objectivity are key to an effective audit. In larger organisations that maintain a dedicated internal audit team, impartiality is less of a concern as the only conflict is in auditing the audit programme (which can be carried out by a suitably trained member of top management or an independent third party). In smaller organisations where internal auditors may be drawn from existing departmental staff, the audit programme should ensure that an auditor never audits their own work.

Internal audits should be conducted by trained personnel who understand both the Standard and how the

---

[17] ISO 27001:2022, Clause 9.2.2.

organisation has implemented its ISMS. Any reputable training course, such as IT Governance's Certified ISO 27001:2022 ISMS Internal Auditor Training Course, will impress upon participants the need for objectivity. Audits must rely on facts and evidence, not subjective impressions or suppositions.

Finally, the Standard requires documented information as evidence of the implementation of the audit programme and the results of audits. The audit programme itself should be treated as documented information (particularly in respect of version numbers, etc. so auditors can verify that the correct programme is in use), and you can use a controlled template document as the basis for your audit reports. You should retain the audit reports for the duration of your recertification cycle (three years).

Management review

The last part of this section, Clause 9.3, requires the organisation to conduct management reviews of the ISMS at planned intervals to ensure ongoing suitability, adequacy and effectiveness. Management reviews are commonly conducted annually; more frequent reviews tend to add little value due to limited data on which to base decisions, while less frequent reviews create the risk of long periods in which the ISMS is ineffective or performing poorly, placing the information it is intended to safeguard in jeopardy.

Management reviews must contain specific inputs. These are listed in 9.3.2 and include changes to the ISMS or the requirements of interested parties, the results of risk assessments and the status of the risk treatment plan, and the status of actions taken at previous management reviews. This is not a list you can pick and choose from – each management review must address all the listed inputs. The simplest approach is to treat each input as a meeting agenda item, allowing the meeting agenda and minutes to serve as evidence that all the required inputs have been addressed.

Compiling the data necessary to cover all the required inputs can take time, particularly for larger organisations. When preparing for a management review, you should allow enough time to collate and analyse the data you will need. You should also take care to present the information in a clear, concise and accessible manner, avoiding jargon or heavy technical details.

If you are responsible for preparing information and/or presenting management reviews to members of top management, you should avoid explicitly or implicitly pre-judging that information. It may be tempting – and even accurate – to suggest that, for example, persistent nonconformities in a process means that more personnel or training are needed correct the problem. However, those judgements are for top management to make, and pushing too hard for a particular outcome can hamper your chances of achieving it. Provide input if asked, but otherwise allow top management to draw their own conclusions from the data.

The results of the management review must include decisions about continual improvement and any changes to the ISMS that are needed. Actions that arise from the management review should be fed into the continual improvement process (covered in Clause 10 of the

Standard), tracked to completion and evaluated for effectiveness. Records of management reviews should be retained for at least one full recertification cycle to serve as evidence for surveillance audits and must be treated as documented information.

10 – Continual improvement

Clause 10 contains requirements for continual improvement. Continual improvement is a requirement of all ISO management systems, and uses the data gathered under the monitoring, measuring, auditing and oversight requirements defined earlier in the Standard.

Clause 10.1 sets the stage by requiring the organisation to continually improve the suitability, adequacy and effectiveness of the ISMS. This is achieved in two ways: through opportunities for improvement identified during the management review process (Clause 9.3), and through the nonconformity and corrective action process (Clause 10.2).

Nonconformity and corrective action

No management system maintains 100% conformity over time. Organisations evolve and change to meet the requirements and challenges of new business, and the management systems they operate must change with them. Nonconformities are a natural and expected part of running a management system, and they do not mean that the system is failing to meet its objectives – only that some parts of the system are not operating as they should.

Nonconformities are usually grouped into three categories: major, minor and opportunity for improvement (often shortened to OFI):

1. **Major nonconformities** indicate the complete absence of a requirement (e.g. no information security risk assessment process), prolonged or wilful failure to meet requirements, or total failure of a component of the ISMS (e.g. an audit programme exists, but no audits have been carried out for six months).

2. **Minor nonconformities** indicate requirements that are met in part, but that suffer from some non-critical deficiency that will not actively harm the operation of the ISMS (e.g. an out-of-date document was found to be in use, or a procedure is missing a requirement).

3. **Opportunities for improvement** indicate minor deficiencies that do not currently pose a problem, but that could become a problem in the future, and general improvement opportunities identified through the management review or during normal day-to-day operations.

ISO 27001 does not formally define these three categories of nonconformity, but their use is established practice by most certification bodies across the world and adopting them provides a useful link between your own internal nonconformities and those issued during certification or surveillance audits. This is not to say that you cannot develop your own categories if you feel it appropriate, but doing so could cause unnecessary confusion. Nonconformities are usually identified through the internal audit process, but they can also arise from monitoring and measurement results, analysis of logs, or other scenarios that highlight deficiencies in the ISMS.

When a nonconformity is identified, the organisation must act to resolve it. These actions are called corrective actions, and they are the core continual improvement function in all ISO management systems.

10.2(a) says that the organisation must react to the nonconformity (no pretending it doesn't exist), then act to control and correct it and deal with the consequences. Listing 'act to control and correct it' and 'deal with the consequences' separately may seem like a needless distinction, but resolving nonconformities is often a multi-stage process. This is true for all management systems, but particularly so for an ISMS.

For example, a failure of a key security control might result in a data breach, making it necessary to deal with regulators, national authorities or data subjects after the core issue with the security control has been resolved. Nonconformities arising from a zero-day vulnerability might involve short-term actions such as temporarily disconnecting infrastructure from public networks and longer-term actions to resolve the vulnerability or replace the affected equipment. The Standard expects you to manage those 'consequential' actions with as much diligence as the initial response and uses the distinction to make this clear.

Corrective actions are not just sticking plasters to be applied to a problem and then forgotten. A key part of effective continual improvement is identifying the root cause of nonconformities and taking action to prevent recurrence. This necessarily requires an investigation proportionate to the nonconformity in question: major nonconformities and those that expose the organisation to significantly increased risk should have more time and effort expended to understand why they have occurred.

10.2(b) addresses this directly. The organisation must evaluate the need for action to eliminate the causes of a nonconformity to prevent recurrence. It must do this by reviewing the nonconformity, determining the causes of the nonconformity, and then determining if those causes have led or could lead to further nonconformities.

When investigating the cause of nonconformities, it is important to remember that the most proximate reason is not always the true cause. You should always try to determine the root cause of a nonconformity, which often involves working several steps backward in the causal chain. For example, a poorly maintained firewall may initially appear to result from inadequate work instructions given to the person responsible for maintaining it, to which the obvious answer is to improve the work instructions. If the person responsible has so many duties that they have no time to properly maintain the firewall, no amount of improvement to the work instructions will resolve the problem – they need more time or fewer duties, not better instructions.

Root-cause analysis is sometimes viewed as needless effort. People generally opt for the path of least resistance when solving problems, and it is tempting to settle on the proximate cause as a way of providing an easy fix or to avoid ruffling too many feathers in seemingly unrelated parts of the organisation. Yet this is a false economy: if you do not find the root cause, the issue is far more likely to recur, which means expending more time and resources to resolve something that could have been avoided entirely if addressed at the root. Root causes also often contribute to multiple problems and resolving them can lead to significant cost savings versus the ongoing 'firefighting' necessary to fix all the issues of which they are a part.

Root-cause analysis should be approached carefully, proportionately and diplomatically. It often involves following the problem into seemingly unrelated areas of the business, which can put people on edge and give the impression that the auditor is 'looking for problems' to solve. There are no easy ways around this, but auditors should always remember that the goal of root-cause analysis (and all nonconformities) is to make improvements and solve problems, not to place blame or create issues where none exist. Leading with the positive aspects of problem-solving rather than the negatives can help with this.

There are many root-cause analysis techniques that you can use to determine the cause of nonconformities, and the approach you take should depend on the severity of the nonconformity and the complexity of the affected systems. Simple techniques like 'five whys' (in which you ask the question 'why?' to each answer given until you can go no further) can be very effective for process- and personnel-related nonconformities, while more complex techniques like fault tree analysis or failure mode and effects analysis (FMEA) may be more appropriate for identifying the root cause of nonconformities in complex IT systems, where multiple independent failures can contribute to larger systemic issues.

With all this in mind, the rest of 10.2 focuses on implementing and documenting nonconformities and corrective actions. The organisation must implement any actions needed to respond to the nonconformity, review those actions to ensure they are effective, and make changes to the ISMS as necessary to resolve nonconformities and prevent recurrence. It must also ensure that corrective actions are proportionate to the nonconformity they are intended to address – deploying half measures in response to major problems or manifestly excessive ones in response to minor issues is not what Clause 10 intends, and questions will be raised about the suitability of the nonconformity and corrective action process during certification body audits if one is sampled.

Speaking of the process, you will notice that the Standard only requires the organisation to retain documented information on the nature of nonconformities and the corrective actions taken to resolve them (nonconformity reports and corrective action reports), and on the results of any corrective action (i.e. whether the actions were effective and the results of any analysis that led to those conclusions).

There is no explicit requirement for a documented nonconformity and corrective action process, but as it is the primary way the ISMS achieves continual improvement, it is 'necessary for the effectiveness of the management system' and falls within the remit of Clause 7.5.1(b) like many other key processes. Regardless of the size of the organisation, you will struggle to justify the absence of a documented nonconformity and corrective action procedure to a certification body auditor.

Annex A – Information security controls

While the rest of the Standard defines the requirements for the ISMS, Annex A contains a list of 93 security controls categorised into 4 themes: Organisational, People, Physical and Technological.

Organisational controls are focused on the policies, procedures, responsibilities and other organisational-level measures necessary to ensure effective information security. They include the information security policy and other core policies, defined responsibilities for management and those responsible for the day-to-day operation of the ISMS, contact with authorities and other relevant groups, threat intelligence and monitoring, information classification and labelling, identity and access control, and asset management.

Employees are a critical part of the information security equation. The controls under the 'people' theme include pre-employment screening, education and training, contracts and non-disclosure agreements, remote working, and reporting of security events.

Physical controls focus on the physical environment of the ISMS, which is every bit as important as the digital environment in terms of ensuring information security. This theme includes controls related to security perimeters and secure areas, clear desks and screens, utilities, cabling, and equipment maintenance, to name a few.

Technological controls are what most people think of when they think about information security. This theme includes controls on malware protection, backups, logging and monitoring, network security and segregation, development and coding practices, and many more.

The controls in Annex A provide a basis for an effective ISMS, but they should not be treated as gospel. You should select information security controls based on your risk assessment and then compare them to Annex A to ensure that all your risks are covered and that you have not missed anything. You may exclude Annex A controls that do not apply to the systems your organisation operates. If, for example, your organisation does not perform software development, control 8.4 on access to source code, development tools and software libraries can be excluded on the basis that the organisation has nothing against which the control could be applied. These justifications must be documented in your SoA.

The controls are derived from ISO 27002. Where ISO 27001 provides a list that defines the controls and what they are intended to achieve, ISO 27002 provides guidance on the purpose and implementation of each individual control in some detail. ISO 27002 is therefore essential for organisations implanting an ISMS and the Standard is discussed in more detail in the next chapter of this book.

Annex A is not an exhaustive list. You are free to develop your own controls or use controls from other information security frameworks as you deem appropriate, and you are expected to do so if the controls in Annex A do not adequately ensure information security across the full scope of the ISMS, or if vulnerabilities are identified that are not mitigated by those provided in Annex A.

Given the pace of change in information security and IT systems in recent years, particularly with respect to the increasing use and capabilities of AI and related systems, development of additional controls to address new and emerging risks and vulnerabilities is likely to become more common. Although each update to ISO 27001 and ISO 27002 addresses changing technologies (for example, the new control 5.23 on Cloud systems in the 2022 editions), the time between revisions means that the Standards necessarily lag behind the latest developments.

Development of additional controls should be appropriate to the risk they are intended to address. ISO 27001 does not expect you to expend major resources to address minor vulnerabilities; the resource and effort expended should always be proportionate to the issue at hand. Like the Annex A controls, any controls you develop yourself or adapt from other frameworks should be included in the SoA.

CHAPTER 4: ISO 27002

ISO 27002 is an essential companion to ISO 27001. Unlike ISO 27001, it does not contain requirements for implementing an ISMS and you cannot seek certification against it. Instead, it provides detailed information and guidance on the information security controls listed in Annex A of ISO 27001, making it invaluable when implementing an ISMS for the first time. Even experienced practitioners can benefit from ISO 27002, as the guidance can be used to help evaluate the organisation's information security controls, reducing the risk of control-related nonconformities and highlighting potential improvements.

Introduction

The nature of providing extensive guidance related to information security controls necessarily involves the use of specific terminology. To minimise the risk of misinterpretation, ISO 27002 provides a list of terms, definitions and abbreviations used throughout the Standard in Clause 3.

As a guidance standard, only Clauses 1–3 of ISO 27002 share the same layout as ISO 27001 and other ISO management system standards. The introduction discusses the value of information security and information security controls in a broad sense, alongside the need to determine controls and organisation-specific guidelines that add value to the ISMS. It highlights the benefits of taking a lifecycle approach to information security, acknowledging that security requirements change and evolve throughout the lifecycle of the data held by the organisation.

Clause 1 outlines the scope of the Standard – it provides a list of generic information security controls that can be used not just in the context of an ISMS, but also when taking a best-practice but less formal approach to information security within an organisation. A business that already has an information security management framework in place, but that wishes to extend and expand its security controls, could also derive much benefit from ISO 27002.

Clause 2 is a standard clause that would ordinarily list normative references, but ISO 27002 does not rely on terminology or concepts from other standards and as a result, there are no normative references provided. Clause 3 provides definitions of terms and abbreviations used throughout the Standard to ensure clarity.

Clause 4 explains the structure of the rest of the Standard, and describes the themes, attributes and layouts of the controls that follow.

As noted earlier in this book, the controls listed in Annex A of ISO 27001 and described in detail in ISO 27002 are categorised into four themes that describe the broad area of security they are concerned with: People, Physical, Technological and Organisational. Compared to older versions of the Standard that categorised the controls into specific security areas (such as access control, asset management, communications security, etc.), the broader approach provided by themes is more accessible to those without extensive IT or security knowledge.

Each control in ISO 27002 is also associated with five attributes. These are:

1. Control type (preventive, detective, corrective);
2. Information security properties (confidentiality, availability, integrity);
3. Cybersecurity concepts (identify, protect, detect, respond, recover);
4. Operational capabilities (e.g. asset management, secure configuration); and
5. Security domains (governance and ecosystem, protection, defence, resilience).

Attributes are provided to allow users of ISO 27002 to view controls through one or more specific lenses. You may wish, for example, to look at all detective controls, or to look at all preventive controls in the governance and ecosystem domain. One way to facilitate this is by creating a spreadsheet containing all the controls and their assigned attributes, then filtering for specific attributes or combinations of attributes.

Annex A of ISO 27002 provides more information on using attributes, along with a table that lists all the controls and their attributes. It also discusses creating your own attributes, both for the controls in the Standard and those developed by the organisation.

It must be stressed that use of attributes to view controls in different ways is purely optional. Attributes have no impact on the controls themselves and no relevance to ISO 27001 certification – their purpose is to provide easy-to-use, granular categories through which to view controls. If you prefer to simply work your way through the controls from beginning to end and ignore the attributes entirely, you are free to do so.

Information security controls

Clauses 5–8 contain the controls. Each one is supported by a table showing the applicable attributes, a description of the control, an explanation of the purpose of the control, guidance on implementing the control, and in some cases additional information deemed useful by the authors of the Standard.

As an example, let's consider control 6.3 on information security awareness and training. Examining the table, we see that it is a preventive control associated with the confidentiality, integrity and availability properties. It falls within the 'protect' concept and within the human resources security capability, and is part of the 'governance and ecosystem' domain. If we were to view the full set of controls through any one of these attributes, we would come across this control.

The control itself discusses appropriate education, training or information about information security and regular updates on the organisation's information security policy for all personnel. Staff should also receive regular updates about any other policies and procedures relevant to their job function. The purpose of the control is to ensure everyone in the organisation understands and fulfils their information security responsibilities.

The guidance that follows notes how the awareness and training programme should address the organisation's unique policies and operations, the information that it holds and the controls in place to protect that information. It says that training should take place periodically but does not specify how often (as that is for the organisation to decide), and points out that awareness training should be provided when a person joins the organisation, and when an existing employee moves to an area of the business with notably different information security requirements to their current role.

It addresses the forms that awareness activities can take and goes into specifics about what an awareness programme should include. It discusses how awareness programmes for highly technical teams need to differ from those provided for less technical personnel, and describes ways technical personnel can maintain their security knowledge outside of a formal awareness programme.

Finally, it notes that it is just as important to cover the 'whys' of information security awareness as the 'what' and the 'how'. Understanding why information security is important underpins everything learned in awareness and training sessions: without that understanding, the measures personnel need to take to ensure security can be seen as 'box-ticking' or needless bureaucracy, undermining their effectiveness.

Annexes

ISO 27002 contains two annexes. Annex A demonstrates how tables can be used to view controls and attributes, and how an organisation can apply filters to view controls in different ways. Annex B contains tables that map the controls in ISO 27001:2022 to those in ISO 27001:2013 (and vice versa) to help organisations transitioning to the new Standard understand where controls have been merged or split into components of other controls.

FURTHER READING

IT Governance Publishing (ITGP) is the world's leading publisher for governance and compliance. Our industry-leading pocket guides, books and training resources are written by real-world practitioners and thought leaders. They are used globally by audiences of all levels, from students to C-suite executives.

Our high-quality publications cover all IT governance, risk and compliance frameworks and are available in a range of formats. This ensures our customers can access the information they need in the way they need it.

Our other publications about information security include:

- *ISO/IEC 27001:2022 – An introduction to information security and the ISMS standard* by Steve Watkins, *www.itgovernancepublishing.co.uk/product/iso-iec-27001-2022*
- *The Cyber Security Handbook – Prepare for, respond to and recover from cyber attacks* by Alan Calder, *www.itgovernancepublishing.co.uk/product/the-cyber-security-handbook-prepare-for-respond-to-and-recover-from-cyber-attacks*
- *IT Governance – An international guide to data security and ISO 27001/ISO 27002, Eighth edition* by Alan Calder and Steve Watkins,

Further reading

www.itgovernancepublishing.co.uk/product/it-governance-an-international-guide-to-data-security-and-iso-27001-iso-27002-eighth-edition

For more information on ITGP and branded publishing services, and to view our full list of publications, visit www.itgovernancepublishing.co.uk.

To receive regular updates from ITGP, including information on new publications in your area(s) of interest, sign up for our newsletter at www.itgovernancepublishing.co.uk/topic/newsletter.

Branded publishing

Through our branded publishing service, you can customise ITGP publications with your company's branding.

Find out more at

www.itgovernancepublishing.co.uk/topic/branded-publishing-services.

Related services

ITGP is part of GRC International Group, which offers a comprehensive range of complementary products and services to help organisations meet their objectives.

For a full range of resources on ISO 27001 and ISO 27002 visit www.itgovernance.co.uk/shop/category/information-security.

Further reading

Training services

The IT Governance training programme is built on our extensive practical experience designing and implementing management systems based on ISO standards, best practice and regulations.

Our courses help attendees develop practical skills and comply with contractual and regulatory requirements. They also support career development via recognised qualifications.

Learn more about our training courses and view the full course catalogue at *www.itgovernance.co.uk/training*.

Professional services and consultancy

We are a leading global consultancy of IT governance, risk management and compliance solutions. We advise businesses around the world on their most critical issues and present cost-saving and risk-reducing solutions based on international best practice and frameworks.

We offer a wide range of delivery methods to suit all budgets, timescales and preferred project approaches.

Find out how our consultancy services can help your organisation at *www.itgovernance.co.uk/consulting*.

Industry news

Want to stay up to date with the latest developments and resources in the IT governance and compliance market? Subscribe to our Weekly Round-up newsletter and we will send you mobile-friendly emails with fresh news and features about your preferred areas of interest, as well as unmissable offers and free resources to help you successfully start your projects. *www.itgovernance.co.uk/weekly-round-up*.

EU for product safety is Stephen Evans, The Mill Enterprise Hub, Stagreenan, Drogheda, Co. Louth, A92 CD3D, Ireland. (servicecentre@itgovernance.eu)

www.ingramcontent.com/pod-product-compliance
Lightning Source LLC
Chambersburg PA
CBHW042315210326
41599CB00038B/7139